More Praise f[...]

These poems are poetgraphs, deco[...]uctions of the cliches associated with pictures. Lee Meitzen Grue's poetgraphs are precise, sometimes delicate and most often power-infused renderings of a sensibility moving among people, moments of history, architecture and neighborhood spaces, flavors , the music and epiphanies. The book must be read as a whole, as an evening of jazz improvisations. Poetgraphs unlock the essence of design and magic in New Orleans, the spirituality of a place where community is created and reborn. The rhythms of thick descriptions force the secular and the sacred to dance in balance.

—Jerry W. Ward, Jr., author of *The Katrina Papers: A Journal of Trauma and Recovery*

These poems take place in the oldest neighborhoods of New Orleans, where the city's soul is to be found: Treme, the French Quarter, Faubourg Marigny, Bywater, and the Katrina-stricken Lower Ninth Ward. The past is mapped onto the present, as memories of an old ice house on Chartres Street and the youngest Marsalis brother "learning his trade in a bar at midnight" flash back even as "the Gray Line tourists come to see the new Pompeii" and the speaker elegizes a mounting toll of departed friends. "I brought the wrong people / to the right place," she laments in a poem about taking three culture snobs from New York City to hear a superb local saxophonist whose name is unknown to them. But anyone whose soul truly resonates to the music of New Orleans will be grateful for this gritty, teeming, life-affirming book—Grue's finest to date.

—Julie Kane, author of *Jazz Funeral*

A city's downtown is traditionally where the action is—it's where people come together to work, play, compete, live. In Lee Grue's wonderful new collection of poems, Downtown, we witness the intricate and fascinating nature of Lee's city, New Orleans, and we meet the people who live there in all their complex glory and joy and sadness. Downtown is where the action truly is—Downtown is where it's at....

—Lowell Mick White, author of *That Demon Life* and *Long Time Ago Good*

Lee Grue knows Treme, Way Downtown, Bywater, Hind Quarter, the French Quarter. She knows the poets and the jazz musicians. She sings New Orleans, and she sings it true.

—Jane Ciabattari, president, National Book Critics Circle (2008-11)

DOWNTOWN

Lee Meitzen Grue

Trembling Pillow Press, 2011
New Orleans, LA

Downtown

by Lee Meitzen Grue

Trembling Pillow Press

New Orleans, LA   .

ISBN-13: 978-0-9790702-42

Typesetting and Design by Megan Burns
Cover Design by Dave Brinks
Interior Photographs © Kichea Burt
Author Photo © Kichea Burt
Special Thanks to Geoff Munsterman for help with typesetting.

Trembling
Pillow
PRESS

http://tremblingpillowpress.com

To Andi,
Enjoyed our conversation
at the Book Group.
Best,
Lee

Oct
2011

Downtown

Lee Meitzen Grue

Lee Meitzen Grue

DOWNTOWN

List of Photographs

I. **TREME**

Lundi Gras
In the Garden
St. Claude Avenue Sweet
Walter Washington: The Wolfman Moves

II. **WAY DOWNTOWN**

Women Carrying Water
Survived: A Hank Williams Album at Fats' House
Sixteen Years Old
Muse in the Attic
King
Fats Domino
Ed's Skate Land: Chalmette
In the Dance Hall of the Mind
Pilot On the Mississippi

III. **BYWATER**

Young Men in Wheelchairs
The Dog Lady
Marbles
Late Sleeper
Feeding the Pictures
Butchie On the Edge at BJ's
Paul Chasse
For Eluard On His Birthday
Mid-life
Kermit Ruffins and His Barbecue Swingers
For Men With Beautiful Mouths
Bad Dream
Ernie K Doe at The Spellcaster
Down In the Bywater
Midnight Train Crossing Lesseps Street

PHOTOGRAPHS

1. Little People's Place, Treme
2. Industrial Bridge, Lower Ninth Ward
3. BJ's Bar, Bywater
4. Cafe Brasil, Marigny
5. Gold Mine Saloon, French Quarter

DEDICATION

This book is dedicated
to
the people of New Orleans,
and particularly,
to my friends and neighbors
in the Ninth Ward
who have suffered
and still suffer,
but always to great music.

DOWNTOWN

TREME

Lundi Gras

Little People's Place: 1992

It's any Monday night.
Red beans and rice on the stove.
About nine o'clock the uptown boys
come with their black instrument cases
filling up the floor.
A young man in sweats slides
to the juke box   sings along.

Davis sets up his keyboard. Somebody
checks out Kermit's photograph on the wall.
Davis plays over the juke box — loud.
The bassist picks up.

These boys
are ready. Some woman makes a selection.
Elliot fronts
some quarters. Half-a-song. *Unplug it.*
What'd you say?
Unplug it.

Kermit's got his horn.
Mouth screwed up sings
some sour tart.

Things warm up when
Marva's Mama starts to second line.
She does a bump with a man
about twenty-five.
Does a hump with a man about thirty-five.
Sashays to the bar for her beer says,
My daughter don't like me to do that,
but I got life.

Kermit sings *Big Fat Woman*
and everybody sings *Little Liza Jane.*
Kermit blows cutting the rest of the band.
His Mama says, *That's my son.*
The keyboard thumps. Davis
shakes his scrappy chin whiskers
like punting on the Thames.

The blues *ragazzi* from Bologna sweat
black leather jackets,
New York Judy sips berry wine coolers
jumps to what
she didn't know before.
The rest share quart Bud.
Nobody cares for nothing
but red beans and brass.

Walter Payton slips in after his gig,
pulls bass until a couple of buddy cops
come in like earache at 1 a.m.
and shut us down.

It's the first careful Lundi Gras
of anybody's lifetime.
We all shuffle over
to Copastetic Bookstore

where somebody had just read a poem
with *nigger* in it.
Folks are walking around stiff-legged,
although the poet says, *I got a right to say it.*
                                    I got stabbed in the eye.

Ah Mos the owner says, *That word don't bother me.*
                                    You got a right to tell it.

Nobody's happy with what's happening
on the street or the man running for governor
who used to wear a sheet, and what's this jive about
the music being too loud?

So everybody moves over to Sidney's on St. Bernard Avenue
where the Rebirth Brass Band sets up and starts over
because nothing's going
to kill this jazz.

In the Garden

in memory of the poet Tom Dent

New Orleans
has too much water
most of the time.
It snakes around us, boils
and thrashes the willows,
breaches the levee,

pours in April, muddies dancers, seeks
cracks in slates, broken shingles, runs
down walls.
Through gutters overflowing
seeks its level, in May
drowns us in underpasses.

It rains and rains and rains.
It's pouring.
                    But shh - shh.
It's quit.

In June we thirst,
hot pink crepe myrtles bloom,
marigolds burn up,
the garden needs watering.

How precious. How rare
Tom's words now
burning like tears down our
dry faces.

Just a few words on a dry street.
Oh, gentle, gentle, rain, his

slow cadences collect in slow drains.
Force us to think.

The source is not the mouth,
the source is the source,
part of the big river.

St. Claude Avenue Sweet

Cars in blue shades, throbbing, shuddering rap-tuous babooms
down St. Claude beating

smoky busses blazoned: St. Claude to Lizardi, St. Claude to
Refinery,

fuming over the corrupt, incorruptible — the strung out body of
Saint Claude,

who lies nodding in Treme, past St. Augustine's, and Elie's
courtyard where

reclusive poets call from high skirted porches, chant litanies and
conjure.

The church swallows loas, all saints sweet.

The big peasant rests at the crossroads:

Esplanade near Polaris, the spinning North star.

St. Claude's lone talkers stalk the littered banquette, ecstatic
prophesiers sermonizing

in raggedy clothes, breathy air dreaming to better things in
unlikely places:

King Roger's: Pickled Tips, Hot Sausage, Cowan, and Coon.

Beard's Auto Repair: No catting, no loitering, no crack, the Hi
Ho, the Saturn Bar,

St. Roch Market: Plate Lunches, Blue Crabs, Boil Crawfish.

Friday in the sometime catholic city. Get Your GED.

In the yard of the fan shop at St. Claude and Elysian Fields

a woman offers BJ's for two dollars, goes

down for a bag of potato chips: Crack. Crank.

This too is life.

At Press Street,

children pass over and under boxcars, daring wheels to turn.

People in cars wait for the train to pass, impatient

circle dust off the gravel road, cut to beat the train.

A long mournful whistle begs them: Don't cross. I'm coming.

Tell me, Babe sang, Don't you want to go?
St. Claude hangs out in the yellow pages — Texacom
Nome Credit Union, the Whitney Bank, and Mandich's:
Got downtown pride and corpus derelicti
Caged grocers count out change, Hank's Po Boys
in white paper, take out Chinese in styrofoam,
Rainbow houses, boarded up houses, things
falling down,
shot up and drive by: Frederick Douglas and
Washington school, and won't things
get better sometime soon. At Frederick Douglas
the principal locks out the tardy.
Medics pick up a body in the hallway on St. Claude.
On Mardi Gras Day
Indians of the Yellow Pocahontas Tribe
dance over the bridge, down the Avenue.
Make way for the chief?
Shaking his headdress
he's come to sing for his mama.
Her name is Alma.
Past Desire, Piety, Pauline, past my house on Lesseps to Poland
Avenue
where St. Claude's ancient knees lift over the levee,
Bridge up drivers take a slow breath,
a moment from the day to watch the boats pass,
and far down there by Harry Sterling
incorruptible toes stretch into the lower nine
past the Louis Armstrong Elementary School
where the fat man Antoine Domino lives in the pink,
smack dab in the middle of his old neighborhood
where people call each other by name, and they call the saint.
They call him

the St. Claude Pharmacy, the St. Claude Handy Hardware.

They call him everyday, but there are not enough prayers to call
him back.

St. Claude Avenue is walled by the dispossessed,
one pay check away from homeless
as new residents sing out:
Gentrify! Gentrify!
We'll B & B ourselves Disney.
St. Claude needs a miracle. Needs one bad.
On the broad Avenue good people abide.
To sustain glory in the name of the people we must all abide.

Walter Washington: The Wolfman Moves

Now the Wolfman's got his teeth,
shines them at Tip's.

Walter you lit us up without
at Dorothy's Medallion Lounge on Orleans Avenue.
Even James Baldwin went there listening.
Some lights you can't hide
even in a crab scrambling basket.

Last night those slides
snake-hipped around your
News.
Headlights flashed in our eyes.
Ears split.
Some punk in your funk,
almost like needle skips.

Everybody asking, What's the matter with, Walter?

Hey, baby, Walter's an artist.
Always going to be trying something.
Everybody's going to try it.
Nobody else going to do it.

We shiver,
hands up—wave clap
and freeze. Scream, Walter, Walter, Walter.

But what gets our shaking imagination
don't get us in the gut.
What moves is still the blues.
Plaaay the blues, Walter.

WAY DOWNTOWN

Women Carrying Water

The well away from the house,
a black pot on a wood fire to boil the clothes, five years old
I carried water in a sirup bucket.
Carried water to help
fill the kettle up to wash the clothes.

Women spend forty billion hours a year carrying water.
Like ants down murram trails in Uganda,
down dry roads in Mexico, dust rising with their feet,
women carry water.
A trickle from a single pipe in Mississippi, women

carry water. Twenty families drink from one pipe in Mississippi.
Son says, I'm tired seeing you haul water.
Bound to be better over there.
She says, Can't leave home.
Some do, he says and leaves.

Over there it's better or worse or just the same,
women carry water.
The water is close, there is no water,
they move on to where there is water
and the family holds on. The family holds on

like ants under the leaves
when the rains come
and there is too much water.
All over the world women carry water
in tin cans on their heads, in camel bags, in

two buckets on a yoke over the shoulders,
women carry water. Women carry water.
Here in an American city,
years after the levees broke,
women carry water in the Lower Nine.

Survived: A Hank Williams Album at Fats' House

There used to be a place called Jewel's on Decatur Street,
a country Western bar; Hank Williams' voice poured out
onto the sidewalk any time day or night you walked by.
In front were men in black leather, hunched over idling bikes
like buzzards, like Hank hunched over the microphone.
Handcuffs and chains hung from their belts. They were ready
for love and love meant pain.

Now, anytime Hank's clinched voice draped in chill truth
rolls out of the car radio I tend to look back on my precious
 moments with a jaundiced eye, dredging up loss as wide
and deep as the broken levee in the Lower Nine
where the barge came through, where two women once
lived with their laughing children in a high house
under the hill until one left dying, wasting like Hank,
whose suffering collected in his throat like rain
water to pour over people who forgave him
for the bitter truth:
that any love is loss, that people who can't swim drown,
that hands can't quite reach the boat, that when we can't leave
what we love to save ourselves we drown, that love is deeper
than pleasure and beyond pain, and if you're
willing to bear it, accept that no love ends happily,
that we can't keep our children from burning their fingers,
drowning in floods:

You'll get the message from the man in the back
of the black cadillac: Whiskey and pills won't deaden the pain
unless you're dead, you love in spite of pain,
and sometimes lie down in a single bed alone.

Sixteen Years Old

she stood clasping him
on the thin wood floor
of her mother's house,
as the wind roared through the barge board door
and water under the sills
slipped the house off
its piers,
until it floated like an old cork
on a river ocean,
and she clung to her son
as if he was life itself,
the only thing hers,
her life had been
nothing
made something by his birth,
she clung to life for his sake
and lifted his precious body
above her head as the water moved them along
until they were washed
against an oak's leaning branches
dragging the river for bodies.

Somehow,
she who did not swim lifted him
and pulled her own body into those limbs
where they became part of the tree for two days
until a boat came
with three men who claimed them,
and a young man asked her how she'd survived,
how she'd saved him
and she said:
I had to, I'm the baby's mama.

Muse in the Attic

At first they didn't know where she was,
just missing … in the crawl space a long time.
The water gone, old man Hebert
already building his house new.

Rolled up in a ball she stayed there.
Couldn't shape pain to words enough to stand it.
One of the lucky
ashamed.

Her nights were floating bodies, racing water,
a girl child torn away
the father able
to save one not the other.

A Lab and a cat left in a house
two bowls of food and water
the family
coming back in three days.

A man forced on a bus
left a note
on his mother
dead in her wheel chair.

Up in the attic, locked in,
The Muse couldn't hear voices.
It was horns playing on the street
finally brought her down.

King

The uncertain notes of Down by the Riverside hang
over the heads of my children marching
in the Lower Ninth Ward,
the horns tilt up singing
to a crowd with teeth.

Some of the teeth smile,
some of the teeth snarl, uneasy
as an animal just free,
too long in a cage.

My children crane their heads,
look over their shoulders to see
if I'm still there — why I ask this of them,
this march for something or someone —
a charcoal image — a face on tv
returning each year, endlessly
repeating, *I have a dream…*

I tell them stories:

Six years old I run to the front door
to answer the bell. A lady
asks to see my grandmother.
I run the full length of the house, out the back gallery,
all the way to the kitchen.
My grandmother is old, moves slowly
to meet the visitor.

Someone says, *You told your grandmother*
a lady was at the door. It's some wash woman off the street.
You shouldn't bother her like that.

I knew a lady when I saw one.

Downstairs at the Wilbert Movie Theater
I scratch fleas under my socks.
I think there aren't any fleas in the balcony,
want to sit there but can't.

At my nanny's house I listen
to the radio in a rocker my size
with a blue-cotton cover tied
to axe whittled arms made
for some dead master's child.

Dr. King released me.
I master no one and no one
masters me.

They tried:
Said my dancing was common,
my mouth smart.
They reined me in to keep me safe,
make a lady.

They couldn't fool me,
I knew about bondage,
from my whittled chair.

I write what I see.

King spoke:
All the petty pride of the genteel poor, poor
as their servants passed from me
in the brown river of his voice.

As the marchers weave and snake
in this year's parade, I wish,

before they cut him down,
the peace keeper could have told us
a new dream for our children.

For anyone who listens
the music is not loud enough
to drown the rumble:

millions of bellies growling.

Fats Domino

at the Blue Room of the Roosevelt Hotel

Velvet ropes and green peas,
a round table at ring side
in the lush, hushed blue darkness
where ice cubes collided in gin fizzes and Sazerac cocktails.

Murmuring waiters served me and my date,
a male hustler, who specialized
in the wives of men who liked to watch.
Respectful of my near virginity,
he was a hip country boy polite as Elvis,
didn't smoke, drink or curse, looked like Chet Atkins.
He'd brought me for something he'd heard elsewhere,
something special:
>The best band in town, Dave Bartholomew's band,
>Smokey Johnson on drums.
Fats was no where to be seen among the white diners.

Some clean, strut young black men set up,
bright and horned for Bartholomew
who kicked off with a hard brass sound
nearly blew us out of our chairs. We were that close.
Fats came in with a careful walk, sat down chunky
and quiet until the spot hit him, turned his face to us,
set his teeth square in a beauty queen smile,
and hit us with
Blueberry Hill. We couldn't sit still.
Hustlers know how to dance.
It was better than a date with a straight man. I let go
and didn't know where I was until five years later
when they let me into The Drop

where I caught the last act
and said,

I've been here before.

Ed's Skate Land: Chalmette

Mr. Willie guards the till,
a cigar stuck in his smile.
One ticket buys the privilege
opening
a door to the Imperial Waltz
where a ball of myriad lights
prisms the floor,
pink blaze, green shadow flying after.
This is the hall where
remembrance is made.
A slender boy holds the waist
of a girl,
his right hand tight at her backbone,
his head cocked.
She is the handle of a dream
through which he is spinning,
this is the waltz without effort,
the walls blur,
nothing between them
will fly beyond this spiral.
They are the eye around which winds
reel
if only,
if only,
the music would continue,
the record turning,
the needle locked.

In the Dance Hall of the Mind

the dancers are gone,
but they still slow drag
in the dance hall of the mind.
They're the best dancers, for them
no regret, they never left.
Tracked water into all night bars,

danced barefoot on wet tile floors
while seventy-five mile-an-hour winds
rattled the beer signs outside:
Trailed out to a soggy morning
as the sun rose up glorious
on slate roofs and sweet olive.

For years the winds eased on past us
knocking Florida to the ground.
A few people uptown took a vacation, but
Flee? what a silly idea! One time the middle as a body
went to Mobile, the storm followed them there,
all the while the French Quarter sitting pretty on high ground.

Once the mayor got fifty thousand people
out of town in cars, a few old people
died, stuck on the highway.
The Mighty Nine said, *Who wants
to sit nine hours on I-10 to get to Baton Rouge.*
Big Joe said, *We ride it out.*

After the marshes went down in the Gulf,
the weather woman talked up storm surge,
people bought axes at the hardware to chop through the roof,
after they went for batteries and water at the drugstore.
Nobody acknowledged change.

This time, the old went into the attics,
forgetting that the sweet drafts of AC
ceased singing through the ducts when the power died,
and the power was the first to die.
Don't be afraid of a little water. We're all about water.
You can swim can't you? And they all stayed put.

Love and loss lean heads together,
hold hands in the back seats
at the Chalmette Cinema.
One woman from Australia, convened at hell's convention,
fed a sick woman her last meal.
Home again, they ask, *Rhoda, how was your holiday?*

The wife, of a friend who writes for the paper,
says to him, *Don't go down there. Don't go down into the valley.*
He has to: Distortion of the familiar is like a sore toe.
You have to look at it and poke it to see if it still hurts.
The Lakeview you knew stables the night mare,
the horse you ride in terrible sleep gallops day time

past Mid City houses with bathtub rings,
Caddies hanging in splintered trees.
The Gray Line tourists come to see the new Pompeii.
Our old Madame with the heart of gold
will take their money. She has to live somehow.
Now that we've lost our toys, we know how much it costs
to love.

Anything you win you can lose.
Our new selves take great pleasure in small triumphs,
clean water and a hot bath.

Pilot On the Mississippi

for Captain C.S. Smith on the occasion of his retirement

The river is there behind the levee.
What seems the same is water, a ship.
A pilot knows
the river, movement and change is
his art.

A pilot
on the bridge of a ship: Greek,
flying a Liberian flag of convenience.
The ship's Captain
nervous as they bear down
on a barge at dock. Now

a lost engine
150 thousand tons and high river, sudden
variables
strings to play
a monster bass. Play it right
or cymbals crash and raw steel

moves a barge through the dock.
On this river ships passing, one whistle — two,
you leave this, turn your back,
stand
on dry land.

Earth too rolls,
the river will not leave you,
watery nights will take you down

to cross ranges deep in the channel.
You know where she's shallow, boils

thoughtless, eager to flow on
with or without you, always and forever moving.

BYWATER

Young Men in Wheelchairs

discarded plastic cups, and Church's chicken bags
roll along St. Claude Avenue.
Nomads
fierce and proud
flat-feet shuffling endless asphalt
or hang dog,

crawling
turf conquered by some new war lord.
A bullet in the head kills, a bullet
in the spine adds another
two-wheeled wanderer to the streets,
regular but slow.
War doesn't end in cool death or hip life,

it ends with you
scrounging like a dog in a garbage can,
scoring a blunt from a fine legged wonder
who laughs and calls you, "My main man," as you
wheel off on a snail's trail home
to Mama

waiting to change your diaper.

The Dog Lady

Tell me, Sarah, how many dogs, cats, birds,
and other serious creatures
mill in your doorway silently according to their hearts?
Scraggly dogs loping sideways follow you,
arrogant cats in smelly doorways
delicately sniff your papery fingers.

Lady, when you tell a joke
do the dogs laugh, the cats scream with pleasure?
Small tongues of little green lizards
moisten their pale mouths
as they race around your pillow,
but they never speak of the green shade of the leaf.

Near mute we speak
swirled in the flow and murmur of our own voices
like frantic fish rising and falling kiss
the walls of the aquarium,
imprisoned in a see through cage
until the flesh falls weeping from the bone, but
Sarah,

dogs follow you home.

Marbles

We find
everytime we dig
pocked agates
milky white
as the eye
of a blind man
cracked blue

along the walks
I work geraniums
out of the dirt
my fingers raise
ancient glass
dim as a fish bowl

in this yard
the earth moves
in slow measured rolls

I met a man
crooked as a ginger root
who said
he was the boy
who played in this yard

if so
there's more concerned here
than time

a fine hand moved
to split them all
for keeps

Late Sleeper

            for Teal

The boy sleeps in deep feathers under the wing,
his foggy mouth dampening the down pillow.
Lifted by quiet breath leaves tremble on the rain tree.
The sun, belly full, lolls
on the floor of his room.
The night swimmer's legs
dream burdened, sink like lead weights.
A mocking bird worries the gray cat.

No lost time,
this sleep gathers, swells, blooms.
The boy's eyelids open slowly
stare:
A perfect black fly, drunken and slow, hums,
washing his hands over the coarse radiant sheet of morning.

Heavy afternoon
yawns into street lights burning in the daytime,
games of red rover. Daddy,
blue pant legs
sprawling on the front step.
Mama, hands in her spread lap, holds
a heavy flower, a white trumpet
blowing perfume into her wide summer skirts.

Feeding the Pictures
for Jim Sohr

My friend the artist does plumbing,
carpentry. Odd jobs for money.
He works in the cold. His fingers
are knobs. The hinges of his knees
creak and crack like ice thawing.
He works in the heat. Sweats
money, salt, gall.

He brings gall home to his wife.
It's bitter, but feeds the small part
of her soul.
The pictures live in a separate house.
At night he is with them in sweet delirium
feasting
on pigment, turpentine, form.

But this house is too little.
They sharpen their teeth,
grow fat on small rodents. Get bigger.
My friend calls them:
They lick his hands, turn up their bellies
to be scratched.

His wife watching from the big house grows jealous.
He likes them better than he likes her.
One picture whines, scratches at her screen door.
She curls her lip, throws hot water on its back:
scalded, shivering, his art starves on the step.

She opens the screen to kick at it, but
it sinks its teeth into the miserly part of her,
swallows her up to the hip in one gulp.

All the gentle words spoken by the artist to his pet
are not the meat that this is. This is food for art.

If you're hanging out in the gallery, eating cheese, drinking wine,
be careful now, it's a big picture, taking up a whole wall.
Don't catch its eye it could swallow you whole.

Butchie On the Edge at BJ's

We don't know what he's on the edge of
could be interesting, maybe
not.
Butchie's probably been edgy
most of his life,
connected to sweet soulful
ness he's a magnet: Draws musicians.

You can sit at BJ's all Friday night, drink beer, and listen,
or *Dance, damn it!*
Get out and dance!

He and Billy Ding of Billy Ding and the Hot Wings
harmonize, Billy on keyboards and vocals,
Butch unplugged. Kenny Holladay jumps in,
speaks in tongues on electric. Mike,
the poet's drummer, is in the mix and
Little Freddie King's side man. God knows
who's there in the back: Trombone?

This is the Hot Wings Big Band. All drawn here like pins.
Butch down front wearing his straw hat, Austin style.
Stage less — he's playing his guitar and singing to us close
Over the Rainbow, not innocent — later.
So hard sweet he makes me cry.

I hope Butchie Trevette is around for awhile.
We love him — his voice.
In the hard morning light, from my porch I see him pass
on the way to the grocery store to get a little something
to keep going.
Hold on, Butchie! Hold on.

Paul Chasse

Where does life go when it goes out?
Is it still here a comfortable chair
we stumble over in the dark?

Words spilled now frozen in our minds
each word redolent
singing out its heart.

Paul who won love
by sending, his words
so strong they carried her home to his house.

Paul, who shot his refrigerator,
making us laugh when refrigerators
were the last thing we could laugh about.

His face suffered loudly, at a time when
there was so much suffering,
it was hard to single his suffering out.

This is no summing up of Paul,
of his kindness there's too much
to report

only a deep sadness
that we won't see his wild
irreverent bike revving up — tearing out.

No pain on the highway.

For Eluard On His Birthday

Dear friend, Aquarius,
this has been the most watery year
of all the watery years I've known you.

Forty days flood, night
blood in biblical proportion.
Astrologers consulted stars,
trembled as planets aligned,
called in dark the name we seldom call in light,

and the flute stood upright in the corner,
ears alert to your breath, the flute knows
nothing without your breath.
My own words hung listless
at the threat of no music,

thirsty children called for water,
your own children stepped up older,
but your wife willed breath back into you:
There is power in love.
Remember the boy who played in barrooms?

The cheeky one who snagged Chuck Willis' turban,
and cut Chuck on his own record
with a sax solo on C.C. Ryder that still won't stop.
He's gone now. He is sound,
the silken breath of Fez and Marrakech,

full throated
washes slowly, rolls back, until
some day distant, ends
with the dignity of a jazz dissolution

on a grace-note.

Read at Eluard Burt's Funeral
August 17, 2007

Mid-life

She drinks
black coffee and picks
at scabs.

One morning
he steps in. Stunning
in his newness, a gift from the gods,
he rents her son's old room,
longs for the mother he's too grown for,

gives her flowers, drives her anywhere,
can't contain himself. Words leap from his tongue:
Old hurts, betrayal
not his silence yet.

This is no cinnamon candy heart, she says! *It's*
half dead, wet, and slippery.
You'd have to yank it out.
Not that strong

he hangs on her words,
thinks she knows. She thinks she knows too much,
can't say: *This hand cleared locked bowels.*
It was my breath that tried to raise the dead.

There's no cake, just too many birthdays.

But the young man buys her a new drink — close dances,
calls her *the birthday child*, begs
just to see her breasts.

For her there's no easy redemption.
No quick fix.
She loves him.
She knows if she sleeps with him
he'll soon forget her — a costly decision.

For six years he comes back.
Sometimes at night
calls from Haiti — calls from Japan

At Mardi Gras pleads: *Don't forget me.*

Kermit Ruffins and His Barbecue Swingers

at Vaughn's on Lesseps St.

Sausage!
Good before you get there.

Smoked meat on Lesseps Street,
trumpet and drum rolls
out the door
on the people who can't get in

that way. *I tell you you can't get in*
that way:
The drums set up.

Sausage sizzles in
a pick up truck.

Kermit cooks.

You can interpret that
any way you want:
Kermit cooks.

Trumpets: *I'm a viper. You're a viper too.*
Sings:
When you're smiling - when you're smiling.
The whole world smiles with you.

Say, *Watch my beer.*
I got to go
put my garbage can up.
Somebody
been stealing garbage cans.

Oh, man, who wants a garbage can?

     Maybe somebody don't have one.
     Watch my beer?

French bread wrapped
on a sausage hunk. *Come
get some*, says the big man
to beer drinkers spilling on the street.

Where the beans?
<u>*Where*</u> *the beans?*
in the back on a hot plate.

I got here at nine.
     Man, where you from?
Milwaukee.
     Band don't set up 'til 'leven.
Paper said nine.
     Don't matter what the paper say
the band don't set up 'til 'leven.

Three a.m.
The man from Milwaukee
eats his beans and rice,
shakes his head: Says,

Nobody at home
is going
to believe this!

Kermit cooks.

For Men With Beautiful Mouths

Darling, your mouth is wildly misused.
You eat off paper plates,
drink from plastic cups, say ordinary things
to ordinary people.
Such a beautiful mouth
should lap
mother's milk from the delicate thimble
of a woman's belly, declare poetry, hasten butterflies
over the thighs and plant deep kisses
on lips that kiss back,
a deep rotation that moves the world
inside.

Bad Dream

Before first light,
behind my eyelids I see our street

empty and dark,

our front gate's iron jaw opens wide,
my small children stride out
round arms, gleaming with fine hair
swinging as they walk.

The wound I keep so well confined
within my chest
opens her tender mouth

cries out:

Watch for cars, look for exits,
don't catch the eyes of dogs that don't bark.

Ernie K Doe at The Spellcaster

in a cold satin frock coat strides
into the crowd like Moses parting the red sea,
five stretchy legged women in briefs strike poses, his
glazed eyes hit blind light,
as he picks up the mike
an electric current gathered from the people
surges through him,
charges us like a lightning bolt burns
the audience to a pitched fever
of moans, freezes, and shakes,
waves them forward and back, jumps
to the sign outside where *Dora's Grocery* swings
over St. Claude Avenue with the news:
St. Vitus in the house teaching us to dance
soul back into our bodies.

Down In the Bywater

on my front porch, July 4th,
hanging out between BJ's and Vaughn's block party,
red, white, and blue stragglers passed.
Over on the corner by BJ's bar
they were shooting off
bottle rockets by the dozens,
baby dolls, spinners
and those rainbows that fall from the sky,
as the night
was lit
with the light of many fires that couldn't last.

Charlie Miller came by after his gig
and we asked him to get his horn and play one song.
A bony guy on a motorcycle came by trailing firecrackers
and stars
too noisy for any tune to pass,
then it was quiet, I looked up and you were at the gate
asking, "Can I come in?"
I said to Charlie, "Play, *I Only Have Eyes For You.*"
and he did.

Midnight Train Crossing Lesseps Street

grief descending
thrills
the night gorge
fragmentary moment
coded in mindful muscle, instant sorrow
tellingly told
lips whispering *around*
the bend, around the bend

on, out of the city.

Who? memory won't tell,
over the river
dead in a ditch
on and on hopping freights,
what was told retold
in the sorrowful moans,
lost love cry
piercing
the night, boxcars gondolas boxcars
gone, gone, gone....

A Few Things Recovered

In a shop where they strip wood in lye vats,
odds and ends,
                    doorknobs, hinges, shutter bolts.

Useful bits to carry
hard nosed
back to our bower.

At the bottom of a box
a towel rack caked with paint,
a shingle nail scrapes it back to the original hue

bought now for the joy of layers
cream, mariner's blue, acid green
thick on brass and wood.

Now
we lay down
fresh paint, quarrels, kisses, varnish
our lives to walk the long hallways.

In our tile bath
unsoiled towels hang straight,
unused by the hands of a child
who ran his hall
new.

Easter

My house full of chrysanthemums
trying to continue. They stand in dry dirt,
expecting something of me, sun or shade,
I don't know which. If I knew enough about life
to find a good place for them
they'd come back again.
How brave.
The refrigerator's full of eggs, slick
and mottled. Mute as violets.
A birthday, Good Friday, Easter and another
birthday. Days follow each other as they should,
and letters I never write
follow each other
in my head. Dear Fred, Dear Alice, Dear David,
dear, dear me.
My mother once wrote:
If my right arm should happen to fall off
I'd never hear from you again. She's right.
It has. Gallows humor, they call it.
A quick grin stretched over the bones.
There's evidence
of winter here in spring.
This morning the knees of my children
cracked like kindling, but overnight
the cat had three kittens. A good sign.
Where did all these messages come from?
I didn't read them.
Every day I wait for the mail. When will it come?
A letter like a ship.
Where is it from?

More and more questions and I less quick to answer.
Today I took to water. Let it wash me away.
When the tide came in I heard Babe Stovall play:
Let the circle be unbroken in the sky. Lord, by and by,
holding his steel guitar behind his blue cap,
he played it in my head
surely someone so shiny is still here.

In the Moment

For the parachutist from "The Times."

Witness,
roll over and tell me again
about oiled camels in Kuwait,
bloated flotsam washed up in Bangladesh,
Afghans with rifles, caves in the mountains.

Tell me. Why were you *persona non grata* in Romania?
Again — how you hid in a closet
to catch Havel in underwear.

When you called from Haiti — whispering,
so dramatic,
you said,

I'll be there — sometime — maybe…
if I can bribe my way out.

Here you are and we
balance: You
with a camera, I
with a pen. Both
junkies for the intense.

Together
in your arms we died.
Open wide — breathe.
Still alive!

HIND QUARTER

Tuesday Night On Frenchmen Street

between
cool tiles
and the simmering ceiling
the band sets up,

street side I sit at a green table
eating fried chicken livers and pepper jelly
out of a styrofoam box. Curious

some late night part of my brain
is trying to put face to name, voice
to face - Ready Teddy
of Ready Teddy's Blues Show on WWOZ
somewhere on Frenchmen Street tonight.

The band plays
some offbeat slow drag. Goes

on and on. A friend pumps me once
and forever around the floor
like a winded foot organ
in a church with siding.

Across the street - outside
I see somebody - maybe
Ready Teddy. Looks
hungry, hung over,
on a lookout for customers.

I'm one of three. Dolores
takes my three bucks, doesn't
stamp my hand. Says,
I'll remember you.
Beyond restless I wander the street.

At Check Point Charlie's
nobody knows
the name of the band,
at Brasil it's the dark search for Kurtz.

at the Blue Nile I'm now one of six.
Teddy's on stage talking blues, turns flips,
stands on his head.
Sings
Meet Me With Your Black Drawers On.

Teddy, Teddy, Teddy,
there's no body
I want,
no wild night before he leaves:
He left,
gone to shoot somebody's dirty little war
for *Life.*

Teach me, he said.
We can play it like a movie we both like.
Oh, I said, *You be Harold. I'll be Maud.*
He's so conversant with death
he thinks I'm on his plane

going down.

I have a request, Teddy
sing,
I'm Through with Love.

You don't know it!
What do you mean
you don't know it. Fake it.
I do.

The Virginian

turns up on my doorstep. No call.
No explanation.

For years we've been involved
in each other's lives.
Introduced him to his wife. God parent
almost. Now he lives in the woods —

West Virginia — with his wife and kids.
He doesn't say he's run away.
We talk about it. This is a soft spot.
Ought to cut it out. Can't reach it.
Wants to go
out. See the town.

But he's not Huck.
He's Tom.

Willie Lockett
playing at Check Point Charlie's.
Willie usually plays Bourbon Street where
we don't go.
Outside Checkpoint there's

cannabis on a cool wind.
Inside the lower ring everything is crawling in
red-eyed, mohawked, kohled, calamined,
and punk tulle tutued.
A man in a stove pipe hat

calls my name. I know him from somewhere.
An Aussie woman says to the Virginian,

Let's dance.
He's shy.

She won't give up.
Dances in one spot talking,
lit cigarette by my leg.
I say, *Watch your butt.*

The band comes on in shades.
All blues. No smooths.
I dance with the roofer tarred by roof.
The Virginian dances with Miss Cigarette.

Laughter cuts
dark, lips matching head,
a chocolate woman, cloche
clamped on her braids — red.

The guy with the big hat passes to the back.
Touches my arm, Hello. Like he knows me.
I know who he is: Jimi Hendrix
born again and blessing our evening.

Uncensored
a sweet talker from Markey's Bar
spots me. So wasted I'm not sure he's the same
guy I know,
and ask him.

I'm HIM, he says, *That your husband?* Tries
to act like we have a past.
I can't remember his name. *I'm HIM,*
he says again.

Here come the undead
crawling out of caskets:

Detoxed, dread locked, mind-fried,
fierce pierced,
mother rude, and permanently tattooed.

The Virginian says, *I'm out of money.*
Me Too.
We lie. We can't hang.
Outside the roofer and HIM
are smoking behind the bar sign.

I go home and the Virginian
somewhat refreshed
goes back to Virginia.

Frenchmen Street Life: Cafe Brasil

Neon opens to blue, yellow, green. Creosote poles hold up the
sky. Breezes melt evening hazes: *Cool. Who are these guys?* Mr.
Dreds leans his Top Hat. Outside lights come on, gray/dusty
rose. Sax relates — you still hurt me: *I'm all for you body and soul.*
Doors open — The street is A/C-ed cooler than cool tuned
to one-sided love: The song says, *I...I turn away romance.* A cop
car passes slowly, bicycles whiz, horses trot — easy. Moon's
hustling quarters on the corner. Hey, Moon *move on.* Tourists
— crows on a rice field, deep dark blue, mysteries, mixed
light and shadow, a fan patterns somebody's ceiling across the
street. *Anybody home? Nobody* no body. Banana trees, willows
over patio walls, listening: *I could not call you if my heart fell out.
We talked about everything everything. Help me! Will never fall from
my lips.* Fragrant people musk oils, body songs: red — opium,
jazz min: Buggies, cars -cars,cars,slowlybumpertobumperedt
aillight, macrobiotically thin a gypsy woman strides in/out, a
luminescent wake, patchouli trailing. *What's the band? Not the
feature*, just *playing for tips. No tips.* No tips, damn it. *Features's
coming on late: 5 bucks.* Praline's window hungry —sweet pickle
tips collard greens *gumbo z'herbes* long line outside. Drummer
carrying a drum drums, the band hangs on cars talking: *Never
been to New York, been to Atlanta. Atlanta's where it's at.* Copper
earrings on a bald woman. Two men in lawn chairs, legs spread,
arms folded. Jazz in the club, rock in the alley. Open, open to
The Empty Motorcycle Blues, jumps the heart's crevasse, black
jeans & leopard skin: *Bye, Stacy. Bye. Somebody beating that drum to
death. This room is live!* Buggy-round again. *No shit? I'm going home.
Can't stay here.* Sharky-black-and-white DeSoto, *John Patrick Toole
O'Rourke's Bandit taxi. Don't want him. Call United.* Man hands in
air: *Had to get out of there — my ex wife down the street — playing
down the street. My house full of pain — FULL of pain. Hey, man,
you must be a millionaire! Fluticious Saxophone! Here comes Mr. Top
Hat!* Incense burning sweet stick incense burning our sweet
burning senses.

One-Handed Piano Players

In my life two of the wonders of the world
have been one-handed piano players.

My Mama would have said it's not nice
to lump people together
or mention their afflictions. What
afflictions, Mama?
I can't play the piano with two hands.

Wheeled in, with an appendage like a paper weight,
Sweet Emma the Bell Girl,
one Olive Oil arm gangling,
could beat a drum out of a piano and heat
the room — one-handed.
Ankle bells jangling,
she didn't move a marcelled hair on her head,
but her gold earrings danced like gypsies.

On the other hand, Mr. Ed Frank could fool you.
You'd look right at him, and you'd swear
he was playing with both hands. God knows
there was enough music coming out for two or three,
but that one away from you was resting on his leg.

It's enough to make anyone with any sense at all
want to play music just so if you went dumb, or
lame, or blind some little part of you would still be
swinging.

At Mona's

A woman walked into Mona's,
stopped, and began counting.
She counted places at the tables — many
places at the tables.
Who were the strangers
come to dine?
Were they tourists in a long bus?
Were they family?

She was a wren of a woman, though
I don't know how a wren looks.
The wrens I've seen were in books —I think
they're small, dun colored.
She was dark haired
wore khaki pants.
The strangers filed in and sat at the tables.

She sat alone.
I would have liked to invite her to my table.

But she didn't seem lonely — just alone.

Little Footlet

Good, I said, *It's mine and it shall be called*
Little Footlet, son of the artist.
                                    —*George Dureau*

In the sweet balance of the flesh
lives the son of the artist, studious of pleasure,
elegant as bone,
awakening as a sour taste in a sweet mouth
he demands,
but silently

jumps around one-legged,
wrestles love, elbows pain,
stumps upstairs
slides down the bannister
and jumps a horse:
Big ribbed, bony, flatulent.

He is a conquistador,
rides like thunder into the night,
such a small secret hidden away,
marches out into the kitchen
makes French toast, hamburgers,
neck bones and greens, settles in to watch TV,

a difficult guest, stays longer than
three days, begins to stink like fish.

Oh, Little Footlet, what some people do
in the name of love.

Helen Hill

To lose this person is like losing a vertebrae.
Today's paper said, *The city falls to its bloodied knees.*

Some people glow from the inside
with a small steady flame
they go about what they do
with certainty.

They choose well. Marry for life.
Children learn from them.

They are not charismatics who draw us into flames.
Helen's fire was banked to last.

Close to us she was one in a list of dead
since New Year's Eve.
We are losing a generation:

Displaced young men without education, without jobs,
their only commodity
crack on somebody else's corner.

If you need work or have no where else to go
there's promise here.
New Orleans is the new frontier.

We are fighting the war of the old West.
How was it won?

By homesteaders who persevere
and bring order at great cost.

Snug Harbor

for George Brumat

After the flood he was right back in place
taking care of every thing and every body.

Gone now: The large space of his life is unoccupied
like a boat's sail where the wind rushed out.

A quiet host, he fed us, let us in upstairs on great music,
surely, he must have gone on to better things.

We gather, with jazz made by friends, to own up
how the loss of one is much in this community.

George, like all the noble purveyors of art, was a healer.

His gift is more of the same in that place.
Our sorrow: How much we miss his face.

For Arnold

Today is my youngest son's birthday.
He's gone. Moved off a month ago.
Today I'm full of tears and regret,
not only at his absence,
but a fear he's not quite finished
like a pie crust not baked enough.
A sorry craving constricts my throat
I want to bind up old wounds,
put band-aids on the past,
shore up the sagging parts
of my life,
already limped away, gone about their business.

But death came sticking his snotty nose in:
An old friend roared off on a Harley New Year's Eve
wearing a funny hat — the token helmet.
His upright old man's back enough to make you forget
the horsepower between his legs.
The last rally — exploded by a truck
on a breathless curve near Acapulco.

For years I made fun of Arnold and he of me.
Each saying the other difficult. Too hard to handle.
But we always talked about the children —
what we wanted for our children.
First time, in my patio the day his daughter was born,
I was hanging out clothes.
he, a late father, asked,
What do you know about kids?

On New Year's day I saw his absence,
things blowing around the interior of his house
like a pressurized cabin with a hole in it,
people slammed up against walls, reeling
and grabbing their throats as if breath had gone out of the
room.
And he wasn't even in residence.
But like his life his death was bigger than.
True this was an untidy end somebody had to tidy up.
First get the body out of Mexico.
$42,200 and a choice of embalmed or ashes.
God, nobody could even imagine him dead.

How could they make those decisions?
His last apocalyptic words
carved in stone:
The chisel into the chest of whoever he said them to.

His children — almost his grandchildren, always
scudding along after his old Volkie hanging onto a chain
for dear life — their skateboards shooting sparks off
the pavement.
Reared with the survival skills of alley cats
and the loose respect for life that
makes old men send young men to wars.
They bear the weight and beauty of his life.
Can I say this in public?
This is about a man — complex — calloused
by seventy-six years, who pushed himself
to the edge, dragging the weakest behind him
falling off.

This is a man whose tragedy was
life was
never quite large enough

for his force or the myth he became.
A man who needed to lead wagon trains West
or doomed treks to the Antarctic, who
needed mountains to climb on the moon,

His dreams led him down rivers already
explored,
and his death turned him into James Dean.

Ellis Marsalis on Wednesday

at Snug Harbor with Jason on Drums

Natalie hangs with the young jazzmen,
knows somebody on the door.
We go upstairs, nod our small acquaintance at Ellis
where he sits on a stool, casual in conversation
with students and friends.

At eleven he goes back downstairs
and sits down at the piano.
Talks into the side mike introducing
Dewey Sampson on bass and Jason Marsalis on drums.

Jason looks like the kid whose orthodontist
has stretched rubber bands from his back molars
to the heels of his shoes,
and when he starts the drums sound just as tight.
This is the kid who'd been loose last year.
Ellis the big Daddy
is really loose, but only in the fingers and it is moving to hear Jason,
who should be bowed down by tradition
and *the live up to your brothers* everyone expects.
Jason just sits there and works — works hard.

Works through adolescence
at a trade, a family trade.

Ellis picks up on a saxophonist and vocalist
from Duluth or Washington or Albuquerque,
they run down from upstairs to take their place on stage
with Ellis, the bassist, and Jason.

At some point a drummer named Cheof comes on
and Nicholas Payton plants himself in the middle
of the stage like a brick house and turns it up,
the drummer who took over in mid set
from Jason is loose but sharp this Wednesday.
You can't help thinking about Wynton, how they used to say
his trumpet had no soul just technique, and the tone
of Wynton's trumpet now,
how what he gives is sometimes fatherhood or hungry children.

There's promise in the stiff clothes of adolescence,
Ellis holding it all together
in those effortless runs
that never seem memorized
and he plays my favorite song
Lush Life and I get back into the music — away from thinking
about the high school student
learning his trade in a bar at midnight.

Dirty Hands

and the Second Hardest Working Man in Show Business

Andy and his sidemen,
a contradiction in terms: Italian blues men.
On drums Kid Caesar,
one of the *ragazzi*, slick black hair, sideburns
and a taste for *On the Road* and Ginsberg.
They're thinking of renting the back apartment -
an efficiency - for three of them the rent is still too much.
Let's face it. Everybody's got the blues, don't nobody
want to have to pay for them.

Dirty Hands at Check Point Charlie's on Esplanade Avenue.
You can hear them down the block,
across the street, three blocks down — across town.
Rock-a-billy? It's loud.

Twenty-four hours the place is full: pool hustlers, laundry doers,
scruffy-jeaned red necks, tattoos and tattooers. Night people
hanging out.
No cover. A tip jug - used to be five gallons spring water -
full of hot air and a few crumpled dollar bills.

Andy is working himself to death joyfully.
I mean joyfully. He's sucking on a harmonica,
jumping in the air, walking on the bar, swinging
from the rafters.
I think what I think when I look at Mick Jagger,
in spite of the life the guy's in good condition,
just watching him makes me cough.

And the *ragazzi* can play,
at first a tick-of-a beat off. Something
we hear in New Orleans some don't hear up North.
Maybe they don't hear it in Bologna.
I think this is going to be like that, but something
happens. Maybe it's the raunchy crowd, maybe
it's the guy called Kenny Holladay, who speaks in tongues
and plays side guitar.

Maybe it's all that energy Andy works up. They get better
and better. Andy pulls out a beat up garbage can lid —
plays it, some harmonica whistle, and a guitar —
plays them all at the same time dancing.
He's got on this bongo black boomerang — drunk
zebra coat.
He's a new age Presley movie in white acrobatic shoes,
an old beret that's set in its ways. I think maybe this guy's too
happy for the blues,
and that makes me sad.
I think this is all too up,
but maybe, maybe baby I'm wrong.

Blues men are always talking deals
with the devil
before you hear the train
whistle and they get on and go away.

Babe Stovall On a Bare Stage At the Quorum Club: 1963

in a blue bebop hat
C.C. Rider...
Oh, see what you done done
You made me love you now your man done come.

Face, irregular and reseamed
like a pair of old jeans,
eyes yellow to the core,
repeats of sneaky pete... thunderbird and muscatel.

On the Square, Babe the street musician
says,
Pass the bottle,
to a shakey guitar man,
drinks out of a brown paper bag
in the city of the go cup.
Babe keens where he comes from, Mississippi. Recent,
his band, two guitars and a washtub
at a no pay party
for friendship, and drinks,
sings about Brown so she's a color and a woman,
picks steel guitar dirt farm
for a bunch of dropouts
who sop up brotherhood like it's gravy
with No War like it's cornbread,

twenty year olds on the floor, parents
of a new born...
playing spoons, beer cans and don't
wake the baby in the next room, plays
as if they - we - can learn where he's been,
see what he's seen.
His raspy voice
strains cords in his neck like
hemp at a lynching, but that wasn't
what his music was,
it was a spread table,
all we had to do was eat.

B.J. is Back

Four women going out.
Three well padded
in fine flesh and soulful clothes,
the fourth fresh-faced and tight-bottomed
in a Lord and Taylor suit.

We're upstairs at Snug remembering:
B.J. sang at a wedding
just come undone,
so we're celebrating and commiserating
with the injured party, in fact,
all of us are injured and undone except
for our little woman who is
so in love.

And we support her,
we all believe.

The audience buzzing, stacked.

On a long tour things tend to fall apart,
wardrobe - hair.

Right away they start:
    What's that on her head,
    Sarah Vaughn's wig?
    Wears that thing like it's an accessory.
    Hmm, Hmm...

The band strikes a match.
B.J. sasses up and down the stage
in high heels, red poppies, tight pants.
sings songs we know.
Songs our lady of the swinging braids
sang in high school.
Songs our separated bride sang
when she torched a silver fox.

Arms lifted we sway, even the little woman
who is so in love right now,
right this minute
moves.

B.J. passes up that note she used
to hit like Ethel Merman
sounds it round
as the pillar in her throat she leans on.
This is not about wardrobe or hair: Slick
or hip. This is about
wounds so deep they don't bleed,
they suck air and sing.

Another voice wails hurt,
B.J. praises the saxophone.
We're so thunderstruck
nobody says anything
until somebody - to break it -

calls out "Dr. Long John,"
because the only place to go

is back to flesh.
She stands out, tells us
about her dentist - Dr. Long John,
who really knows how to fill a cavity.

Now we're talking funky butt,
and the once-upon bride yells,
>   *Yeah, B.J.*
>   *I think he gave you the short end*
>   *of his stick.*
Everybody falls out laughing like this
is the funniest thing in the world.

B.J. switches mood to standard.
Offers up the stage to the next
generation, a generous act
says,
Top that.

A woman - plump, virginal
does a silky Ella voice.
A young cat honeys, "Look at Me," means it.
Shifts
hip attitudes for the camera.
A woman struts up
stuffs a five, fans twenty on his crotch,
her son says, "Oh Mom."
From up here we see the singer's got
a bald spot.

A big wailer from Baton Rouge
in a butt hugging dress

distracts the bass
to the point of losing it.

She's good. The band can play:
But B.J.
comes back undisputed.
Sings "Rocket Love"
like it's a classic blues
and we're all beside ourselves.

We drop whatever there is to say
about a performance and go
off and talk
at the *Cafe du Monde* until 4 a.m.
about love and men
and someone sends a *billet-doux*
to the little one.
We hood our eyes — smile
because we do
still believe in love.

Astral Project

at Snug Harbor

It's late.
Moonlight in Vermont.

Johnny Vidacovich, beer by the bass drum,
towel slung over his shoulder, padded drumstick
a gong in a J. Arthur Rank movie.

Expressive
as a moot question
James Singleton plucks mid bass.
Steve Massakowski's broad face glows
like an oil lamp in an igloo.

Originals.
Long rhythm sections
grounded by tenor sax.

Mid set pit stop: The band
hawks Tee shirts
to make a buck.

Back to business: Hey!
Something new —
Johnny drums up a street parade —
solar bass catches up.

Sax ends with a tear, non-inflated :
Tony Dagradi on soprano,
juice mother to Steve's ax,
a brain-plastic electronic boz box
with green, red, yellow lights looks
intelligent.

The band jumps down
to hang out between sets, somebody plays
Mose Allison on the juke box.

2

On stage skeletal mikes,
the empty piano, drum sleeves
the texture of oranges lounging,
the bass sleeps.
A blue lit guitar leans
against the wall smoking
a menthol cigarette,
silver rings and a black harness
wait
for mean sax in a studly position.

Onstage
the band tunes up like the symphony.
Swings a standard: Cold

martinis and a hot date.
Singleton stops making sense
in his loose talking head suit.
Psychic synergy off
the astral plane

these guys fly
drums and bass in a state of grace.
Inspace the structure as written
on air,
black on white quotes Singleton's suit,
plant cells of the *Daetura*. Line
boxes the rhythm section:
bass, drums, guitar

working on the patterned
ether coming up on a painterly sax

slaps down a broad band of blue
right through the middle
of night streets
past dark shuttered houses,
potholes, high water
streaming cracks in the flood wall. I fly it
home
to Bywater,
my blue gate and my dog
Blue Cheese.

Ade's World: Cafe Brasil

The man stands in the shadows
under the balcony.

He watches
the show across the street.

Light and music, people mill and talk. Neon
fades and curves slowly
more brilliant for its absence.
Hand bills poster the wall, cyclists wheel
return
calling to people leaning on cars.

A woman in a muted green kimono
sits at a table sipping espresso, she too
watches the show and the man
in the shadows.

Rapt
the raggedy people find an edge,
teeter comfortably
in soulful cothes, all part of the set.

The *auteur* tires of his part,
He says, *The old cars are props.*
My whole life is props.
Nothing is real.

He walks in time to the drum,
crosses the dance floor,
raises
his fist in a gesture,
but a littered table is center stage,
he picks up empty bottles.

Kefaru thumbs his heated drum.
This is the scene. Here.
Rapturous changes.

The building radiates: blue, yellow, green
on a face as old as the Quarter,
its ancient back rests on the backs of termites
dying in the trenches, wood dust sifts through their teeth, rises
around the feet of the dancers on Saturday night,
as they stiffen one leg and limp wildly to *Los Bebes de los Merengues*.

and the wild haired man in red and gold and orange
works
to keep it going like a plate
spinning on a stick until, like all worlds
in this wonderful, terrible world of entropy,
it begins to slow
like a tropical eye
in the center a hurricane
calm falls,
motes drift lazily through Sunday afternoon's
summer hat show.

The man buys new tables, chairs, red shoes
for the seemingly inexhaustible dancers
soon replaced at the barricades
by younger troops. They too will someday remember

these moments as glycerin perfection,
when the host of balloons: red, yellow, and blue
limply follow the street musician
as he calls them
on down
the street
with his sad trumpet.

THE FRENCH QUARTER

The Old Ice House on Chartres

In the ice house night
trucks roared through huge doors to the cold.
Big men pinched blocks of crystal with steels claws
flung it up to stacks and stacks of cold
all night work.
                                    Boots stomping, shouting,
hard sheets of their words fell from the walls
like sleet,
and the breath of the men rose around them
like the breath of cattle in a winter field.

At the door to the dark of the ice house night,
                          our eyes just open,
moving from the crush of the wheels of the truck,
we watched them work
while shaking the cubes in our cold glasses.

Tim Green at Rhythms on Bourbon Street

Three New Yorkers in tow,
a couple of writers and an actress.
The man is looking for Bunk Johnson.
I tell him Bunk Johnson is at Tower Records.
You can hear him there tomorrow.

It's too early — too early for Russell's Cool: Kermit Ruffins.

We're the second party in a big patio
sort of place, as I said, on Bourbon.

I'm trying to tell these people about this great
saxophonist.
How lucky they are to get to hear him.
The band is working to an empty room:
bricklayers—workmen laying it down.
What you hear almost any place in New Orleans.
Keyboards, drums, two saxes and a bass player.

The man from New York has that married look.
Bored. Doesn't want to be here.
This is not Bunk Johnson. This is live.
The actress is reacting.
You expect her to get up and sing with the band.

The other woman has downed her drink. A gallon
in a plastic cup. Now she's dancing.
This dance has sores on its legs.
Her nice body feels the music,
but she's drunk and Parkinsonian.

The wrong people: I brought the wrong people
to the right place.
The woman stops dancing. Sits across from the man.
The music is too loud to talk.
They wouldn't talk anyways.
She cries. Sobs. Dry sobs.

Tim steps forward and begins to blow something
to do with all this,
but his own.
He plays off the band, around the band, he plays
off the big empty room with-red-neon-Monteleone-sign
outside iron work, trees with Christmas tree lights.
Tired messing around with you, oh, baby.

Plays everybody's number on the radio dial,
makes you shake,
move your hips, makes you feel

the low moaning inside everything.
Stopped in it like traffic, like jam:

The lighted skyline,
bored man, crying woman, and a restlessness
in the cha-cha, boogie-woogie actress who is
moving us
to the next place, the next man, another horn,
Russell's Cool down in the neighborhood
where you shouldn't use your phone outside
on the corner to call a cab unless
you want to get shot.

Closing China

The AC shuts off at 4:30 am
an alarm
basting me in my own juices
I know something has changed
look at the clock:
It's later than I thought it was.

Yesterday's slow fumble drops a bowl,
rice pattern, bone china,
on a tile floor beautiful
things break.

Someone calls: The bad news:
The Chinese-American on Royal Street is closing.
Good news: Still there: today and tomorrow.

We come with our goodbye presents
some customer already there with a video camera.
The old man stiff with anger.
His wife smiling, joyful: *Old friends,*
she says,
How's your daughter? she asks. The same question always,

We're sorry. We'll miss you.
Where will I buy some plates? My gifts?
Here is my son, she says. Handsome with his cell phone.
Here is my daughter. Cropped hair, shorts, a sweat shirt.
Where do you live? Chicago. Houston.

I buy the last three rice plates and water flowers.
No incense, finger traps, sparkly, twirling stars,

no lanterns, hapi coats, fertility rabbits,
no more **What's better than one fish? two fish.**
Where are the recipients? *Gone to graveyards.*

Insight
the sudden heat
that makes you throw off the covers sees:
There is no beauty in the window but a blue/white teapot
at a discount.
My friend lingers fingering left over boxes.

Sorry, the old man says. *We're busy. Go now. Closed*
Nothing left. This is trash. All gone. She apologizes.

Jade on a top shelf: Too rare to buy. Sell

At the Gold Mine Saloon

the poets sing of love and death on Thursdays,
the podium stands solid on time layered,
separate doors to a brick stable
where jazz musicians
dark and light passed through
to play together.

This is history.

The proprietor, a stocky poet with a boyish face,
reads coded poems to peers on Thursdays,
weekends he's a DJ on a dance floor
where collegians twirl crystal fantasies:

Quarter art, TVs, and old video games.
A wordplay of the eye irresistible to
the irreverent, who gather to throw
their words against the walls.

The mighty few who come to listen.

The Fire Eater

tilting the bottle up
drinks kerosene like it was
whiskey
then passes forward and back
with the flame
held
on the torch of his hand,
his head moving
like the head of a cobra, his hand
moving to his mouth
lips touch
and he catches fire

the audience drops back
he moves up
the steps of St. Louis Cathedral
like Jesus
      in a miracle
I walk past in my red jacket
for a long   hot look
wanting to spit coals back at him
as he moans   mama
and his tongue shoots flame
under the white hem of my skirt
a slow curl burns in an updraft

I pass downwind
the fire
smoothing my skirt   a charred
ring of crisp muslin   a bit of soot
on my left shoe

Potatoes

For all those lost at The La. Pizza Kitchen

make good soup, crumbled bacon
and cheese on top,

sometimes cold, elegant
garnished with parsley, disdainful
of beginning in dirt.

In a magazine reproduction, Van Gogh reminds:
The poor
are always with us. *Potato Eaters*
gather
near

where the potatoes were dug,
dirt still clinging
to their poisonous green eyes,

which I carefully peel away,
carelessly tossing the potato-water
onto a plant in my kitchen,
watch it wilt, and in a few days
die.

This morning's
stark headline, details
of lost extraordinary lives, ordinary potatoes
stuck on the mouths of guns,
mouths silenced at 10 a.m.

and suddenly I taste dirt.

The same taste in my mouth
another time - a newspaper article - the potato
shoved in the mouth of a woman
to silence her,
a nameless soldier's
cruel need forced open her thighs,

and I know
any good can be turned to evil
by mistake.
Something alters the simple pattern
that moves us,

turns us instead:

A non rectifiable act
puts the laughing living
underground
and changes men
with guns and potatoes
in their hands

to hope extinguished
in their mother's eyes.

Monument to Pork Chop

I read it in the paper.
"Oliver 'Pork Chop' Anderson died
July 2nd on Lesseps Street in the 9th Ward,"
just six blocks down.
The picture, a long-faced nephew
at odds with Pork Chop grinning prime
on a poster he'd signed to pay his funeral.
Not to be because the Dennis Mortuary on Louisiana Avenue
needed money: There wasn't any. Cold feet

strike no fire. In my mind,
Tom Dent and Danny Barker whisper a bitter chorus,
"Hmm — Plantation time."
But listen Tom — Danny — no shame in Pork Chop dancing.
He wanted to and people wanted to see him.
Artists often die poor,
richest in the work — applause, laughter
can't be banked.

And the Greeks say, Count no man happy until you add his life.
Like a fugue all the voices will arrive.
A headliner — even the woman at the dry cleaners knew
he'd passed lacking money and sick. Her face told it:
There's my youth gone, dead of cancer
in a three room apartment.
She said, *If you find out more, let me know,*
speaking of someone esteemed she's lost track of.
And maybe Pork Chop tapping before we changed the laws
knew:
You can dance out before you can walk out.
That's a property of intelligence,
to know what exists and what should be exited.

Nadia: Underwater on Bourbon Street

She strips herself slowly, underwater
in a tank,
her hair floats up
containing roses, lipstick, chalk.

She rolls upward, wheels over
back arched,
light and shadow wavering,
her face hallowed as the bones of coral.

She is mystery spinning slowly
without breath,
from her hard breast
small wooden nipples emerge.

She is a figurehead
launched in the great waters,
her mouth, the shadow of kisses
on the glass floor of our fantasy.

When she rises, wet haired
smiling, to the surface,
we put her from us as the dead
washed up on a day lit beach.

Lala the Bead Lady

says
>   *A good address is*
>   *where you don't get beat up*

nods

silver hard hat
trampolining the sun
off the cathedral steeple

sings
Buy my beads?
NO! NO! damnyouto hell
PISS OFF!

uptown
>   Lala's uptown
>   on the streetcar going down town
muttering Lithuanian curses
at a nice woman on the beauty seat

did you ever see her eat?

old/young
a certain age
like Dietrich asleep
on the hood of a Mercedes

if you put a chisel to her
she'd shatter
rather than divide

an original
you can't buy
break your lens on Lala
she'll sell you beads
give you lip

but no head at any price

Ingrid Kelly

did not come
to the conclusions of time.
She left us in summer
like those lovely
things
that land on leaves.

So beautiful.
        Too quick.

Poem for Ingrid Kelly on a memorial at McDonogh #15 School

Girls In a Bar on St. Louis Street

We are the knowing virgins,
our long hands, our white arms,
are the dark mahogany reflections of old men.

We are ripening cheese,
strung out faces green
under the beer clock.
We wait in the air-cooled days

for whiskey nights,
the same songs on the jukebox,
a hand with a bar rag wiping
the wood before us.

Faint veins of blue lard our bodies,
we are unhealthy, pungent,
we are the returned for taste,
thick, white, waxy.

We see, afternoons, a rectangular sun
at the door, sipping tall drinks,
we are waiting for the real
music to begin.

Staged dances we dance together,
our arms slide along each other,
cold as the lip of the bar,
back to first position,

the jukebox stops with the clock
out of juice
we kick the wall to start it up,
angle our arms, our legs

into stiff postures for the dance.
We are overwhelmed by a supreme effort
to contain a terrible rage.

We are the knowing virgins
dressed by the cursing wives.
We are the dark stared into
by men who wish to enter us
mistaking our vacancy for youth.

Behind the Beaded Curtain

stares at men and a few women who peer in. They're
more clear than she. They walk on heavy, touristy feet.
Is she real? they ask.
She tells them secrets if
they venture behind the curtain.

Outside, through the door
shadows hurry a sunlit wall, pillowed
by the rough voices of bluesmen, a radio,
racking up the hard words of jaded love, cheating love,
love gone wild, love gone crazy, love gone away

and the woman rocks on
the sun, the voices on the radio, the beaded curtain
that roils in the breeze, the image of Mary

a wavering blue ellipse,
hands folded, pretty mouth pouting
lost chances, an immaculate conception.
Untouched, she sways in the breeze

waves beating the doorframe,
as the woman's eyes follow
in an altered consciousness dreaming
the curtain,
herself behind it.

In the House of Marie Laveau The Palmist Reads Her Own Hand

sees the lifeline is deep but not long.

Here, in the back room
with the green lamp shade,
the reader sits alone, lays out the tarot,
writes in a yellow book. Expectancy
is the center of the room.

For a price - advice.

Up front,
in the shop, chicken feet on sticks,
books, icons,
oils, and masks.
Today, Marie's death day,
a fresh bouquet placed at the
dusty altar - candles.

To the cashier,
a thin man in raggedy shorts
says, *Marie won't tolerate dissension in her house.*
At Mardi Gras when the drunks came in,
she threw the pictures off the walls.

It's hard to keep drunks out
on the corner
of Bourbon and St. Ann.
The Midwest has emptied onto Bourbon Street
leaving room for buffalo
on the Great Plains. Hanging over

New Orleans bars people hunker down,
talk in flat tones.
Today ask the reader for
luck in love. Seek a spasm of forgetfulness.
Want to know, *Where am I going?*

The death card predicts new beginnings.
The client leaves. The room
folds into itself.

In the storeroom
back of the black curtain, cartons
of powdered incense, and
a bathroom smelly for centuries. Next to the sign:
Don't Flush Paper Towels, hang packets:

Maquey, Contra Sal, Roja Sal, Eucalipto, Sauco. Bags of *Quina.*
Man candles, black candles.
High John the Conqueror candles
lined up on the shelf.

Nothing bad
could happen to you there.

On the wall in the reader's air-cooled room,
three pictures from the tarot: The lovers,
the baby sun on a white horse, pentacles carelessly
thrown as coins not signifying money.

And again someone
knocks on the translucent door.

Cut the cards with your left hand,
witness your choice. Your spread
the Celtic cross: priestess ruling, the mystery
of the hierophant,
moon leading with her dark side
into light. Under the cold beauty of the moon
it is most difficult to lie.

On this day, Marie
passed to the other side. Here,
the locus of power
in a spinning centrifuge,

a leaning frame house,
a pitched slate roof shedding
ancient rain.

Erzulie Freda Daome Comforts Old Men and Boys

The ordinary you needs me.
I know the piercing pain of love
receding,
the cold face of the dead lover,
worse, the lover hot faced in other arms.
I know, I know
and I pity you.
It matters not to me
you're old — young, a scroungy
Tom cat yowling in the rain.
I don't care if you recognize love too late
as desire rages, and
your body will not comply.
I love you
as your mother loved you,
if she loved you.
Erzulie clothes your suffering in silk,
balms your fear of death.
If I take up a woman's body
she will melt, care for you
above her hard life, rough hands.
This woman, looks into her mirror,
sees my face. Cloaked in scent, she unfolds you in her arms.
She will not scorn your lost job, sour breath,
the rent gambled away.

Three of us will ride into the night
on the wild horse of love.

Comfort Me with Apples for I am Sick of Love

The mandrakes give a smell,
and at our gates are all manner of pleasant fruits.

As conceived, this love does not smell of indoles from indigo,
compounds that strengthen fragrance, jasmin sambac,
the smell of intestinal putrefacation, the smell that hovers
over carcasses and the old blood of menstruating women.

Come my beloved
Let us go forth into the field…

Sub Saharan truckers cross and re cross the continent, leave
slick snail trails, miles of sperm, trucks carrying death as cargo.
We smoke and dance in the juke joints of the world
where white teeth and laughter warm us to what is good in life.

I am my beloved's and his desire is toward me

and toward his friend he meets in the men's room at the park.
What does your lover's desire carry? What does your belly carry?
an infected child who will wither and die before your eyes
as you who are too sick to care watch helplessly

We have a little sister and she hath no breasts.
What shall we do for our sister?

Exact a promise of no physical love until she is spoken for?
Lovers change the definition of love to suit their fancy,
in countries where the hymen is sacred
love and death enter other doors.

His left hand should be under my head
and his right hand should embrace me.

Why visit nightmares when the dream of another body
fits ours and is sweet upon us? He is strong and beautiful.
Like a cat I would lick his fur. I would comb his fur with my
tongue.
His body is fragrant and pleases me.

And the smell of thy nose like apples...

If your death smelled of death at love's beginning would you
fall into his arms? If the infected smelled foul at first kiss would
you still cling to him thoughtless of continents
emptied of children by lack of attention to one indolent detail?

The mandrakes give a smell,
and at our gates are all manners of pleasant fruits.

In words I would never find otherwise, my poetry emerges from the hynagogic state near sleep.

-Lee Meitzen Grue

Lee Meitzen Grue was born in Plaquemine, La, a small town upriver. New Orleans has been home for most of her life. She discovered poetry and Edgar Allan Poe in a vault full of school books in Anahuac, Texas where she spent summers with the Meitzens. Although she writes about anything that strikes her fancy, Nijinsky and Texas for instance, much of her poetry and many of her stories have to do with place and the place is New Orleans.

She began reading her poetry at The Quorum Club during the early sixties. There she met musicians, Eluard Burt and Maurice Martinez (band leader Marty Most). Burt had just come back to New Orleans from San Francisco where he had been influenced by the Beats. The Quorum Club was the first non segregated coffee house in the South. At that time it would have been unlikely for Lee Grue to meet and work with African American musicians any place else. Eluard Burt and Lee Grue continued to work together over many years. Burt and his wife, photographer Kichea Burt came home to New Orleans from California again in the nineties, where the three collaborated on a CD, *Live on Frenchmen Street*. Eluard Burt passed in 2007. Kichea Burt contributed some of the photographs in this book.

During the intervening years Grue reared children, directed The New Orleans Poetry Forum workshop, and NEA poetry readings in the Backyard Poetry Theater. In 1982 she began editing *New Laurel Review*, an independent international literary journal, which is still published today. She has lived downtown in the Bywater for thirty-five years.

After the flood of 2005 she began teaching fiction and poetry workshops funded by Poets and Writers, Inc at the Alvar Library, which is three blocks from her house. Such fine writers have emerged from this workshop the library is publishing an anthology of their work.

ACKNOWLEDGEMENTS

WORK No. 6: *Survived: A Hank Williams Album at Fats' House,*
St. Claude Sweet (also in The Bywater Newsletter)
Hawai'i Review: *King, Fats Domino*
YAWP: *In the Dance Hall of the Mind, Ernie K Doe at The Spellcaster*
Art Voices: *Butchie On the Edge at BJ's*
Chicken Bones Journal: *Young Men in Wheelchairs, For Eluard On His Birth-
day*
Brilliant Corners: *In the Garden, Kermit Ruffins and His Barbecue Swingers,
Down In the Bywater*
poetry.com: *Midnight Train Crossing Lesseps Street*
Ploughshares: *Easter*
Louisiana in Words: *Frenchmen Street Life: Cafe Brasil*
Three Poets in New Orleans: *One-Handed Piano Players*
Authors Views online: *Helen Hill*
Warren Wilson Review: *Ellis Marsalis on Wednesday*
Xavier Review/Shelley's No. 9: *Babe Stovall On a Bare Stage At the Quorum
Club: 1963*
Mississippi Valley Review: *Marbles*
Deep South Writers' Winners Chapbook: *BJ is Back*
Louisiana English Journal: *Tim Green at Rhythms on Bourbon Street*
The Double Dealer Redux: *For all those lost at The La. Pizza Kitchen*
Ellipsis: *Nadia: Underwater on Bourbon Street*

In the Sweet Balance of the Flesh: *Ed's Skate Land: Chalmette, Marbles,
Little Footlet, For Arnold, Lala the Bead Lady, The Fire Eater, Monument to
Pork Chop, Tuesday Night On Frenchmen Street*

French Quarter Poems: *Babe Stovall On a Bare Stage At the Quorum Club:
1963, The Old Ice House on Chartres, Girls In a Bar on St. Louis Street, Nadia:
Underwater on Bourbon Street*

Other Titles by Lee Meitzen Grue

Trains and Other Intrusions. Poetry Forum Press, 1974

French Quarter Poems. Long Measure Press, 1979

In The Sweet Balance of the Flesh. Plain View Press, 1990

Goodbye, Silver Silver Cloud. (short stories) Plain View Press, 1994

Live! On Frenchmen Street (with Eluard Burt) CD, 2000

Three Poets in New Orleans. Xavier Review Press, 2000

Colophon:

The font used for the text was Adobe Garamond, which is a digital reproduction of the Roman fonts originally designed by Claude Garamond (1499-1561) and the italic fonts designed by Robert Granjon (1530-1589).

The first 26 copies of this book are lettered and signed.

This copy is letter _____.

Titles from Trembling Pillow Press

I of the Storm by Bill Lavender

Olympia Street by Michael Ford

Ethereal Avalanche by Gina Ferrara

Transfixion by Bill Lavender

The Ethics of Sleep by Bernadette Mayer

forthcoming titles

Song of Praise: Homage to John Coltrane by John Sinclair

Maniac Memories by Jim Gustafson

Full Tilt Boogie or What's the Point by Paul Chasse

Trembling
Pillow
PRESS
www.tremblingpillowpress.com

Made in the USA
Charleston, SC
07 September 2011